W9-AOM-893

your friends

YOU KNOW THEM WELL.

BUT WHAT DO YOU KNOW ABOUT FRIENDSHIP ITSELF? TAKE THIS TRUE–FALSE QUIZ TO FIND OUT.

True or False?

1 The friends you have as a teen are some of the most important people in your life.

2 Teens in the popular crowd are usually the happiest in school.

3 Peer pressure is always bad.

4 Connecting online first is a great way for teens to meet new people in real life.

5 Gossip can be a form of bullying.

Answer key: (1) True. Peers help you figure out who you are going to be. Read more in Chapter One. (2) False. Teens in the most popular clique are often insecure about losing their status. Read more about it in Chapter Two. (3) False. Peer pressure can be a positive or a negative in your life. It's up to you. Find out more in Chapter Three. (4) False. The Internet is great for many things, but for teens, meeting online friends in real life shouldn't be one of them. More on Internet fun and safety in Chapter Four. (5) True. Words can humiliate and intimidate—and that is the essence of bullying. More on gossip and bullying in Chapters Five and Six.

Photographs © 2008: age fotostock: 103 bottom left (Fabio Cardoso), 103 top (Vstock LLC); Corbis Images: 93 (Ephraim Ben-Shimon), 4, 18 top (Gareth Brown), 53 (Mina Chapman), 35 (DiMaggio/Kalish), 8, 70 (Kevin Dodge), 24, 59 (Randy Faris), 81 (Grace/zefa), 13, 33 (Charles Gullung/zefa), 56 (Sven Hagolani/zefa), 41 top (Richard Hutchings), 29, 96, 97 (Image Source), 50 (Sean Justice), 18 bottom (Estelle Klawitter/zefa), 37 (LaCoppola & Meier/zefa), 100 (Tom & Dee Ann McCarthy), 79 (Newmann/zefa), 58 (Jose Luis Pelaez/zefa), 55; Getty Images: 49 (Blend Images LLC), 52 (Peter Cade), 27 (Judith Haeusler), 86 (Dick Makin), 43 (Photodisc), 64 (Bob Pool), 41 bottom (Rubberball Productions), 95 (Shawn & Sally Weimer), 12 (Michael Wildsmith), 90, 102 (Yellow Dog Productions); ImageState/First Light: 5, 75; JupiterImages: 68 (Ron Chapple), 89 (Corbis); Monty Stilson: cover; PhotoEdit: 76 (Cleve Bryant), 103 bottom right (Kayte M. Deioma), 6 (David Frazier), 84 (Jeff Greenberg), 21 (Michael Newman); The Image Works: 72 (John Birdsall), 22 (Topham); VEER: 69 (Blend Images Photography), 38 (Digital Vision Photography), 15, 16 (Photo Alto Photography).

Cover design: Marie O'Neill
Book production: The Design Lab
CHOICES editor: Bob Hugel

Library of Congress Cataloging-in-Publication Data
Webber, Diane, 1968–
Your space : dealing with friends and peers / by Diane Webber.
p. cm.
Includes bibliographical references and index.
ISBN-13: 978-0-531-18849-1 (lib. bdg.) 978-0-531-14774-0 (pbk.)
ISBN-10: 0-531-18849-3 (lib. bdg.) 0-531-14774-6 (pbk.)
1. Friendship. 2. Peer pressure in adolescence. I. Title.
BF575.F66W43 2007
158.2'5—dc22   2007006579

1 2 3 4 5 6 7 8 9 10 R 17 16 15 14 13 12 11 10 09 08

SCHOLASTIC
CHOICES™

Dealing with friends and peers

your space

Diane Webber

Franklin Watts

AN IMPRINT OF SCHOLASTIC INC.
NEW YORK • TORONTO • LONDON • AUCKLAND • SYDNEY
MEXICO CITY • NEW DELHI • HONG KONG
DANBURY, CONNECTICUT

your
crew

your crew

THE MOST IMPORTANT PEOPLE

A Guy's View: It's About Trust

Justin, 17, of Illinois, says there are some key ingredients to the friendships that mean the most to him.

"My close friendships are based on similar interests and the confidence that I can talk to them knowing that what I say will stay just between us. They give me insight, and I can trust that there is some confidentiality there."

A Girl's View: We're a Lot Alike

Whitney, 17, of Oklahoma, shares much more than just a first name with her best friend.

"My best friend is named Whitney, too. I've known her for seven years. We met when she was new to my school. She sat in front of me in class, and we were always getting in trouble for joking. We hang out, go to movies together, parties together. We're a lot alike. People call us 'The Whitneys' because we're always together."

How Important Are Your Friends to You?

If you are like most teens, your friends are way important. Not more important than your parents, of course. But given a choice of who you'd rather spend a Saturday night with . . . well, is it even close?

This is as it should be, experts say. **Adolescence**, also known as the teen years, is the time when you begin to move out of your family circle and into your friendship circles more and more. Teens spend a lot of time with their friends, and they spend a lot of time thinking about their friends when they can't be together.

Why? Because you are growing into the individual that you are going to be. "Adolescents are trying to answer two questions, 'Who am I?' and 'Where do I fit in?'" says teen expert Margaret Sagarese, the coauthor with Charlene Giannetti of *Cliques: 8 Steps to Help Your Child Survive the Social Jungle*.

It seems like a **contradiction**, Sagarese notes, because one question is about your individuality and the other question is about conforming to a larger group. But they're related: as you choose your crew, you choose qualities that are important to you. These qualities are based on your values. And your values are the foundation of your identity.

SO, TEEN FRIENDSHIPS?
Yeah, pretty important.

journal it!

Reflect on a friendship you have now or had in the past. Write your answers to these questions in a journal. Your answers may clue you in to how you approach friendships with others.

HOW did you meet your friend?

HOW long have you been (or were you) friends?

HOW is this person different from other friends in your life?

WHAT experiences strengthened your bond?

WHAT experiences weakened your bond?

WHAT is/was unique about your friendship?

Making Friends

Brandon, 15, has known Nick for about as long as he can remember. "I met him because my mom made me go outside," Brandon says. "I think I was about four, and she said, 'I think there's a boy your age playing next door. Come outside and meet him.' We've been friends ever since."

Do you have any friends you've known as long as Brandon has known Nick? Friends who knew you back in the day are to be treasured. Make time for these special connections, so you can keep those bonds strong. You really can't replace that kind of history.

But friends, even best friends, often go their separate ways before they hit middle school. Maybe your best friend moved out of state (see Chapter Four for tips on staying in touch). Or maybe you just developed different interests and grew apart. Either way, many teens form new, close friendships in middle school.

The initial meeting might just be by chance. Like Whitney, you might find your future best friend sitting in front of you in class. Or you might build tight ties with one of your soccer teammates. You could be fast friends, connecting right off the bat. Or your friendships might develop slowly.

Either kind of friendship—one that takes off in a flash or one that slowly blossoms—can be satisfying. If you are open to the idea of new friends, and are willing to share your real feelings, friendship can flourish.

Friendship Check #1

What do your friendships say about you? And do you like what you hear? "The effects of the friendships you have now will last far into your future," says **psychologist** Tina B. Tessina, PhD, author of *It Ends with You: Grow Up and Out of Dysfunction*. Tessina encourages teens to evaluate whether your friendships are positive or negative influences on your life. How do your friends make you feel? Do you feel like they give you support when you need it? Do you and your friends value the same things?

If you don't like the answers to those questions, Tessina says you should make a change. "Find out whose lives are really working, and figure out a way to gravitate toward those people."

quiz

DO YOU
know me?

How well do you and your friends know each other? Go through these questions together and see. Maybe you'll learn a thing or two!

1 What is my friend's favorite movie?

2 What is my friend's favorite thing to do on a free afternoon?

3 Which school subject drives my friend crazy?

4 What is my friend's dream job of the future?

5 What is our favorite topic of conversation?

Boys vs. Girls

Who are friends more important to: boys or girls? Many people would answer with a loud "GIRLS!" But it's a trick question. Tight, close friendships are important to both boys and girls. But that doesn't mean boys and girls behave the same way in their friendships. "Boys' friendships are simply governed by different rules and expressed differently than girls' friendships," writes psychologist William Pollack, PhD in *Real Boys: Rescuing Our Sons from the Myths of Boyhood.*

Pollack has an ongoing project of listening to boys talk about their lives. (You can learn more about it at www.williampollack.com). "Boys often use action-oriented behavior to express their connection to other boys," he writes. Things like hanging out to shoot hoops or riding skateboards are what he calls "caring through action." "Boys connect one-on-one, too, but they usually do this privately, away from the larger group," he says.

"Boys connect one-on-one, too, but they usually do this privately, away from the larger group."

For girls, the deep connections can be more public. Girls tend to form tight-knit pairs and trios. Many spend a lot of time talking about emotions, relationships, and what's important to them. And like "The Whitneys," everyone starts to expect close girlfriends to do lots of things together.

"Friends are a lifeline for teen girls," says Laurie Mandel, EdD, a teacher and the creator of the Get. A.Voice Project, which

"Friends are a lifeline for teen girls."

fights name-calling in schools. "The connection to friends is really **primal** for girls. They are looking for a sense of belonging, to feel cared about. They want friends they can trust."

But there's no reason to get caught up in what friendship "should be." Both girls and boys can add new dimensions to their friendships by learning from others. A pair of friends who normally spend their time together having long talks might have a blast if they go to a movie instead. Two buddies might get a lot out of an afternoon where they hang up their cleats and talk about nothing in particular for a while.

Source: Amanda Lenhart, Mary Madden, and Paul Hitlin, "Teens and Technology: Youth Are Leading the Transition to a Fully Wired and Mobile Nation," Pew Internet and American Life Project, 2005.

BY THE
numbers:

Teen Friendships

22

Average number of friends teen boys say they keep in touch with at least once a week

17

Average number of friends teen girls say they keep in touch with at least once a week

10.26

Average hours per week teens spend on social activity

83%

Percent of teens who belong to at least one school or community club

Another healthy thing to do is to develop friendships with members of the opposite sex. Both Whitney and Justin, whom you met at the beginning of this chapter, have these kinds of friendships. "I know I can trust Nikki," says Justin about his girl pal. "She helps me figure things out." Whitney's best guy pal is the drum major at school. "We've been friends since eighth grade. He's a great guy. I really value our friendship," says Whitney.

Friends of the opposite sex can give you views from a different perspective and help you form bonds with a variety of people. Finding ways to connect with members of the opposite sex can help you in more ways than you might have suspected!

Connection Counts

Psychologist Michael Fowlin, PhD, emphasizes the importance of healthy connections to others. "Teens are struggling to figure out who they are. That **terrain** is often rather lonely and painful, even when you have strong friendships," said Fowlin, who is also an actor and performs a one-man show called *You Don't Know Me Until You Know Me* in schools all over the country. "The kids who are most likely to do things to harm themselves or others are the students who don't have any connections to their peers."

Friendship can be a solution to these frightening problems. "When the friendship is working, you have a sense of belonging, of shared experience, shared pain," says Fowlin. "Teens need that. Everyone needs that."

The teen years can be hard. You don't have to get through them alone.

"When the friendship is working, you have a sense of belonging."

FINDING
new pals

Does your current crew disappoint?
Here are four steps to make new friends:

GET OUT THERE:

If you want to meet some new people, try doing a new thing. Drama club, karate classes, horseback riding lessons—anything you might be curious about, give it a shot. You'll probably need to go three or four times before you get over your nerves and really start to connect with others.

BE READY AND OPEN:

You can strike up a new friendship anyplace, but you need the right attitude. Treat everyone you meet with respect. Ask questions and flash a smile. Be open to letting friendships develop.

GO DEEP:

The difference between an acquaintance and a real friend is usually a few deep conversations. Trusting someone new can be a little scary, but it's the way to take a friendship to the next level.

KNOW WHEN TO MOVE ON:

In spite of your best efforts, a new friendship might not work out. Sometimes, someone you think is great just isn't interested in a new friend. Maybe the person is too busy. Maybe he or she is just not feeling the same click that you are. If a few of your phone calls or e-mails go unreturned, if you're getting the cold shoulder at school, back off for a while. One of two things will happen. Either the person will miss you and start trying to get in touch. Or it might be time to let that friendship fade. Try not to be discouraged. There's someone else out there, someone you will click with. Just keep trying.

CHAVEZ H.S. LIBRARY

your crowd

WHEN THINGS CLICK AND CLASH

The Downside of Cliques: A Negative Environment

Lauren, 17, lives in Florida. **Clique** clashes were a big problem in her school, and they forced her to take dramatic action. "Cliques are the reason I left high school to be homeschooled. People were so mean to each other. Even when it was directed toward someone else, it affected me. I got very depressed. It was a very negative environment, and my mom and I decided I should just leave."

The Upside of Cliques: A New Tone

Courtney, 15, lives in Alaska. One teacher's leadership—and the cooperation of the student body—changed the whole **dynamic** of cliques at her school.

"Our rival high school across town has a ton of clique problems, and we had some, too, last year. So this year we really made an effort to change that. We've tried to be more welcoming to freshmen. They aren't treated like little kids anymore. We did things—like the sophomores switching places with the freshmen in assemblies, so they can be dismissed ahead of us. We're showing freshmen that we appreciate them, and it kind of sets a tone. There are still groups, but everybody gets along pretty well this year."

Group Think

Geeks, goths, gangstas, jocks, preps, nerds, skaters, outcasts. Did I leave anybody out? You betcha. In fact, I've left everybody out. No individual person can be reduced to a one-word label.

GEEKS
goths
gangstas
JOCKS
preps
NERDS
skaters
outcasts

Does your school have cliques? Do things usually work out fairly well, as in Courtney's school? Or do cliques make life a nightmare for some kids, as Lauren experienced?

Sadly, experts say cliques are a problem in most schools. Courtney's school is the exception, not the rule. "All kids are affected by the exclusion, ridicule, and humiliation that are prevalent in schools today," said author Margaret Sagarese.

Cliques have always existed. But Sagarese thinks they are more damaging now than they have ever been. "The broader culture is a culture of cruelty. Kids think it's cool to be cruel because that's what they see all around them in the media," she says. "We can't eliminate the social ladder, but we can call for a higher standard of kindness and compassion in our schools."

33%

About 33 percent of kids are in the popular clique, which is made up of clique leaders and clique followers.

10%

About 10 percent of kids are wannabe clique members. They try to be accepted by the popular kids, but never are fully accepted.

45%

Most kids, about 45 percent, have a few close friends but aren't in the popular group. The Adlers called these groups "middle friendship circles."

10%

Loners, kids with very few or no friends, make up about 10 percent of the students.

The Social Ladder?

Do you understand that term, the social ladder? That's a way of referring to the rankings of groups in a school. Popular kids are on the top of the ladder. Unpopular kids are at the bottom.

Sociologists are scientists who study how people behave. Patricia A. Adler and Peter Adler are sociologists who went into their children's school to study the way the students behaved in groups there. They wrote about what they found in the book *Peer Power: Preadolescent Culture and Identity*. The Adlers and other researchers found that students tend to fall into groups in predictable numbers. (See the chart at left.)

Your Turn

Think about the groups at your school. Do the Adlers' numbers seem about right?

Now think about which group of people has the best deal. Who feels the most confident? It must be the popular clique, right? WRONG. The Adlers' interviews showed that kids in the popular clique, especially the followers, were often insecure. Followers might be picked on and made fun of by clique leaders, who need to establish their power. The clique leaders, for their part, get power and respect—but sometimes they aren't genuinely liked.

POPULAR CLIQUE ≠ confidence

"Those who have the **social currency** have further to fall, more to risk," says Laurie Mandel, creator of the Get.A.Voice Project. Members of the popular crowd at Mandel's middle school "are happy as long as they have a bunch of friends. The number of friends is what they value, as a sort of exterior measure of their **status**," she says. "They want to be wearing Abercrombie or Hollister. They need these external signs of status."

Sagarese agrees that popularity has pitfalls. "They're always watching their backs," she says. "They are afraid of losing their status, so they can be very insecure. A bad hair day can be a catastrophe."

Research shows the top rung of the ladder can literally be a dangerous place to be, too. "They're more at risk for substance abuse and early sexuality because they attend more parties where this kind of thing is going on," says Sagarese.

"They're always watching their backs."

Does all this mean that popular kids are miserable? Not at all! It's definitely nice to be liked by a lot of people. The risks of popularity really come from situations where kids are putting their social status before themselves.

The truth is, if you try to be something you're not, just to be accepted, people usually see right through you. While "just be yourself" may sound like a cliché, you'll find that pretending to be someone you're not will never make you happy. If being yourself makes you popular, you're ahead of the game. If it doesn't, at least you're being honest, and those who like you will have more trust and respect for you than if you were putting up a front.

BE yourself

Wannabes and Loners

Wannabe kids don't have it easy, either. They wonder, "Where's my self respect?" Sagarese writes. Wannabes are looking for acceptance from people who might be toying with them. They'll drop a real friend in a second if someone from the popular crowd calls. But the wannabe never gets full acceptance into the popular crowd.

They stay on the fringes of the popular clique, however, because they might not have anywhere else to go. If a wannabe has abandoned a true friend to hang out with the "cool" kids, everyone may see him as a suck-up.

Not surprisingly, loners are the kids who have the toughest time of all, at least in school. They might be the target of bullies, and their isolation might leave them with a lot of anger and sadness. Some people just aren't good at reaching out and connecting with other people. Taking risks in the teen social world is terrifying, no matter who you are. And some people

wannabes

are more sensitive to this than others. It takes guts to reach out to someone who seems very different from you, but you may be surprised at how much you have in common and how refreshing a new point of view can be.

WALLFLOWERS
in bloom

Here are some celebrities who battled shyness when they were younger:

Alexis Bledel

Brad Pitt

Alison Lohman

Carrie Underwood

Mia Hamm

Anna Paquin

Courteney Cox Arquette

David Letterman

Jim Carrey

Julia Roberts

Tom Hanks

Make Room in the Middle

Where is the healthiest place to be on the social ladder? The Adlers and Sagarese say it is in the middle friendship circles. Those lads may not have the popularity, but they have the loyalty and security. So they have higher self-esteem and a better self-image.

Mandel points out another advantage of those middle rungs: perspective. "Girls who are not in the popular crowd have a very interesting perspective on it," she says. "They see the betrayal that happens in those groups, and they are happy to have one or two friends that they really respect."

YOU

Where are you on the SOCIAL LADDER?

Having friends from different groups gives you flexibility.

The Adlers point out that kids in the middle friendship circles might feel a little envious of popular kids, who seem to be having all the fun. But remember, that fun can come at a price.

A healthy approach is to claim membership in several groups. If you've got some sports friends, some debate team friends, some neighborhood friends, and some religious-group friends, you've got options. "It gives you flexibility," says the psychologist Tina Tessina. "If so-and-so is mad at me, I can hang out with someone in another group. The more peer groups you are in, the more skills you are learning for dealing with people. That's going to make you happier right now and be useful to you all the way into adulthood."

Can We Change Cliques?

Experts say with some leadership from caring adults, we can change clique culture.

In Courtney's school, it was one teacher's idea to make the school more welcoming to ninth-grade students. "It set a tone of respect for the whole school," said Courtney. At schools where the Get.A.Voice program is in place, a core group of students works with teachers to encourage everyone to think about how negative language and name-calling hurts others. "If there is more than one student saying, 'Hey, that's not cool,' it's less of a risk," says Mandel. "In the face of peer culture, you need more than one person to stand up and say something is not right. I've seen a core group of students and teachers stand up and use their voices. And that starts a wave effect that can change a whole school."

"I'VE SEEN A CORE GROUP OF STUDENTS AND TEACHERS STAND UP AND USE THEIR VOICES. AND THAT STARTS A WAVE EFFECT THAT CAN CHANGE A WHOLE SCHOOL."

Beyond Tolerance

Tolerance sounds like an ideal that groups should strive for, right? Well, maybe it isn't enough. "If we think about it, tolerance is about people from different backgrounds just leaving each other alone," says clinical psychologist and actor Michael Fowlin.

Tolerance is clearly better than intolerance and bigotry. "It's a nice stepping-stone up from **oppression** and discrimination," says Fowlin. "But if we move beyond tolerance, we get to inclusion. We get to a place where we can say, 'Yes, we are different. Let's figure out where we can complement each other. Where are our similarities?'"

INCLUSION

tolerance

intolerance

discrimination

Can you think of some similarities that your group of friends shares with another group in your school? How could you include someone you rarely talk to in your circle of friends?

your choices

your choices

HANDLING PEER PRESSURE

The Upside: Giving You a Push

Justin, a high school senior in Illinois, found the power of positive **peer pressure** on the gridiron and in the classroom. "At the beginning of football season," he says, "I was really looking at other players. I saw who was better than me, and I tried to figure out how to make myself better. I was pushing myself. Academically, peer pressure can work for me sometimes, too. If I've got an assignment that I'm procrastinating on, I've got a few friends who will push me. They'll say, 'C'mon Justin, just get that done so we can go hang out.' It's helpful."

THE DOWNSIDE

The Downside: Revealing the Truth

Brandon, 15, of Florida, says negative peer pressure sends him a clear message. It tells him who is a real friend and who isn't. "There are people who have pushed me to try things. But I don't think they were my real friends. They were people who were just pretending to be my friend to get me to do something. Eventually, I think they got bored with me and gave up. Good friends won't try to push you into anything you don't want to do."

revealing the truth about peer pressure

It's Not All Bad

Talk about a bad reputation. Peer pressure has one of the worst. This is because negative peer pressure is the culprit in lots of teens' decisions and destructive behavior. Drinking, smoking, cheating—all three are things that teens are more likely to do if their friends are doing them. But does this mean all peer pressure is bad?

No! Peer pressure, like cliques, is another one of those facts of teen life. It can be positive or negative. Yes, the peer pressure that gets the most press is the kind that gets teens into trouble. But peer pressure can also help you to get in shape, learn to play guitar, or apply for a job at the mall.

Judith Rich Harris is the author of *The Nurture Assumption*. In that book, she argues that peer groups have a lot more influence over the kind of adult you will become than scientists previously thought.

Harris cites Midwood High School in Brooklyn, New York, as a place where peer pressure plays a positive role. A magnet school for science and the arts, Midwood has a mixed population of students. Half of them take a test to get into the school; the other half go to the school because it is in their neighborhood. But the funny thing is that everybody at Midwood does better in school, as compared to surrounding high schools. The good attitudes of the high-achieving kids who test into the school spread to the neighborhood kids. Ninety-nine percent of the graduates go on to college. One Midwood student, a semifinalist in a

"The good attitudes of the high-achieving kids who test into the school spread to the neighborhood kids."

national science contest, told the *New York Times*, "At Midwood, being a science nut . . . is a good way to make friends, and being ambitious is far from shameful."

Friendship Check #2

Which kind of pressure do you give your friends? Which kind do you get? People are not all good or all bad, but on balance, do you think your crowd is a good influence or not?

These are important questions. And you have the power to answer them for yourself. (Though don't be surprised if your parents have different opinions.) The peer pressure question also strikes at the heart of the question about the quality of your friendships. True friends want what's best for each other, as Brandon discovered.

Justin agrees that there are lines real friends won't cross. "A friend might ask me to do something, but a really good friend wouldn't push me when I say no. He would know when to quit," says Justin.

> "A really good friend wouldn't push me when I say no. He would know when to quit."

real
FRIENDS . . .

are interested in you as a person, not in something you can give them;

value your well-being and never ask you to do something dangerous;

are genuinely happy for you when things go well;

apologize when they make mistakes;

listen and care about what you say;

make themselves available when you need help;

respect your privacy;

don't expect you to be perfect;

like you and accept you just the way you are.

Source: Adapted from *Choices*, November/December 2004.

what about GANGS?

Gangs are one example of extreme and dangerous peer pressure.

Q. WHAT IS A GANG?

A. Sociologist and gang expert Michael Carlie, PhD, defines a gang as a group of individuals who have an ongoing relationship in which they support each other and repeatedly conspire to break rules and commit crimes.

Q. WHY DO PEOPLE JOIN GANGS?

A. Experts say teens join gangs to meet some need that they have. It might be for safety, love, excitement, or money. Sergio Argueta is an ex-gang member from Hempstead, New York. He and his friends started a gang in middle school because they looked up to older gang members in their neighborhood. "I thought I had power," Argueta said. "But I was powerless." But Argueta didn't realize that until he'd lost three of his best friends to gang violence. Two were killed in cross fire; one went to prison for one of the murders. Now Argueta is dedicated to educating kids on the dangers of gangs.

Q. WHAT HAPPENS TO GANG MEMBERS?

A. Many gang members end up dead. Others end up in jail at a very young age. Once arrested, they have an 80 percent chance of being arrested again. Behind bars, gang members miss out on a traditional education. They miss out on a normal life. They lose the power and the freedom to be who they want to be.

Q. HOW CAN YOU AVOID GANGS?

A. The decision to stay out of a gang is one of the best you can make. Safeyouth.org gives the following advice for staying safe when you have gangs in your community:

- Find positive ways to spend your time and energy.
- Stay away from gang members and be aware of gang colors and symbols to avoid being mistaken for a gang member.
- Never carry a weapon.
- Be informed about gang activity in your community.
- Join a group that is working to get rid of gangs in your school or community.

What to Do?

What can you do if your crowd seems to be on a road that you don't want to travel? Try to find a new crowd. You don't have to do it angrily. You might not even have to cut ties completely. Maybe there are a couple of kids in your current group feeling equally uncomfortable. If you talk about it, you can find ways to do other things together. "It's not just about finding connections," says Fowlin. "It's about finding the right connections—groups where it's cool to be smart and it's cool to be good."

Fowlin knows it isn't easy to change direction. It is hard to project yourself into the future. If you turn away from your crowd right now, it might not be easy to see that this is temporary, that you will find a better group soon. He encourages you to think about your favorite movie. "Do you remember that slow part in the beginning before the movie really got going? You had to get through that part before the movie became great," he says. Finding a new group of friends can be similar. Once you have connected with a new group, it may take some time to feel comfortable and in sync.

However, the work you put into friendships makes them more rewarding in the long run and strengthens the bonds between you and your friends. It is in the early stages of your friendships that you really learn whether or not these people will have your best interests in mind. As you develop trust and respect for each other, that's when all your work truly pays off and the story of your friendship really gets going.

your screen scene

your screen scene

FUN AND SAFETY ON THE INTERNET

The Upside:
Protected and Connected

Courtney, 15, feels good about the time she spends online. She protects her privacy and connects with her friends. "I like talking to my friends on MySpace. It's a good way to get in touch with people and stay in touch with people who don't live around you. I like that I can decide who can contact me, and I can **block** people I don't know. It feels private, protected."

THE DOWNSIDE

The Downside: Harassed and Bullied

Thomas, 12, of New Jersey, was in the chat room of an online medieval role-playing game when another player started to bully him. "A kid started to call me names that you can't say on TV," he says. But because Thomas had been trained in Internet safety, he knew exactly what to do. "If you're being bullied on the Internet, stop, block, and tell someone about it."

harrassed
and
bullied

The Internet: Good or Evil?

So which is it? Is the Internet a scary place where threats lurk on every other Web page—or is it an amazing way to connect with friends and share information? Yes, this is another trick question: the answer is that it's both.

"It's a tool," says Nicole Ellison, PhD, an Internet communication expert from Michigan State University. "It can help you have wonderful interactions, or it can be quite the opposite."

SUPPORT
SUPPORT
SUPPORT

The Internet can allow people to reveal things about themselves that they may be too shy to share with real-life friends. "A gay teen who lives in a small rural town might be able to find support online that he can't find in his community," says Ellison.

The Internet can also be a great way for you to keep a friendships going with someone who has moved away. That friend's perspective on the ups and downs of your crowd might be just an instant message away.

"[The Internet] could be a lifesaver for a teen who needs support that he can't find in real life."

These are positives, but not everything about the Internet is positive. Ellison elaborates: "There are two sides to every coin. It could be a lifesaver for a teen who needs support that he can't find in real life—or it could support a really negative behavior that a teen is engaging in."

Just as a teen who is dealing with something difficult—like serious illness or divorcing parents—could find others in the same boat to talk to online, so could a teen who is getting into something dangerous. There are sites that promote hate groups, bigotry, and self-destructive behaviors.

Teens have to exercise some judgment about which virtual groups are safe to join and which would have a negative impact on their lives—just as they do in real life.

"I like that I can decide who can contact me. . . . It feels private, protected."

Nobody Knows Me Here

One of the things the Internet offers is **anonymity**. In fact, experts strongly advise teens to keep all of their personal information private when online. Being anonymous can give you a sense of freedom to express your creativity. And this can be **empowering**. "Bloggers are writing for a larger audience than just themselves," Ellison notes. "With YouTube, you can make a video and have a thousand people watch it."

But anonymity has a downside, too, Ellison warns. There's little **accountability**, so there might be an anything-goes mentality. "Groups can be more likely to engage in extreme behavior," she says. "They might be more aggressive, more exclusionary. So that could lead to painful interactions for a teen."

GROUPS
can be more likely to engage in extreme behavior.

Online Bullies

Another pitfall of the Internet is how it is being used by people who *do* know each other. It is giving bullies another way to pick on people they don't like. And it is a very public form of bullying. "Kids have always been mean to each other. That is nothing new," says Ellison. "But the Internet makes it easier to have a wider audience for this meanness."

Researchers have collected some very extreme examples of cyber-bullying: polls posted to vote on the ugliest kid in school; a bully's target being bombarded by hateful e-mail. Cell phones also play a role. A bully's friend snaps a picture of him pantsing someone in the gym. Then the picture gets e-mailed to half the school. The victim has to deal with the embarrassment of the initial attack—plus the embarrassment of the cyber-attack.

Strategies for Dealing

The important thing to remember about the Internet is that it is a public place. And like other public places, there are rules to keep everyone comfortable and safe (see "Road Rules" on pages 61–63). Don't post anything online that you would be uncomfortable saying to a person directly. Don't post anything in a public space that you wouldn't want your mom or your math teacher see—because you never know, they might go looking. That's what "public" means.

Also be protective of your time spent online. Connecting with people online can be fun, but it shouldn't replace face-to-face interactions, which are more satisfying. If you play games online, Ellison advises you to be aware that the games are designed to get you hooked and keep you playing. "You have to spend a lot of time with these games to be able to do the cool things," she says. If it is impacting your schoolwork or your real-life friendships, you may be spending too much time online.

Do you need a break from the Internet?

If you've really been burned online by a cyber-bully, consider taking break from the Internet. When you are ready to go back to it, open a new e-mail account and be very protective of your identity. You might also want to limit your use to e-mail and school research until you are sure the storm has passed.

Don't be afraid to tell your parents or a trusted adult at school if you feel threatened online. They can help you handle the problem.

ROAD
rules

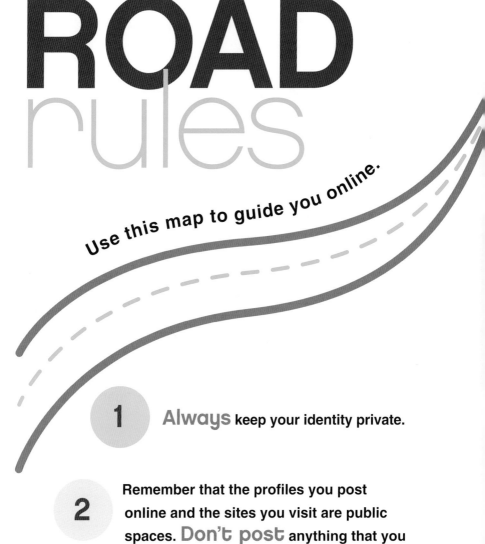

Use this map to guide you online.

1 **Always** keep your identity private.

2 Remember that the profiles you post online and the sites you visit are public spaces. **Don't post** anything that you wouldn't want the world to know about.

3 Never give out your password to anyone.

4 When choosing a screen name, don't use your full name or even part of your name. And don't choose a sexy or provocative name.

5 Make sure that you have an antivirus program for your computer.

6 Never open e-mail with an attachment from an address you don't know.

7 Never get together in person with someone you've "met" online.

8 People aren't always who they say they are. Be careful about adding strangers to your friends list.

9 Just because someone gives you personal information or an e-mail address doesn't mean that you have to give that person your information.

10 Never respond to e-mail, chat comments, instant messages, or other messages that are hostile, hateful, or inappropriate. Harassment, hate speech, and inappropriate content should be reported.

11 Follow chat rules. Know about the chat room before you enter it.

12 Don't post anything that would embarrass you or someone you know.

13 Don't mislead people into thinking that you're older or younger.

14 Talk with your parents about their expectations and ground rules regarding surfing and chatting before you go online.

Source: *Choices*, September 2006: 8. Tips from myspace.com, safeteens.com, and teenangels.org.

your grapevine

your grapevine

THE SCOOP ON GOSSIP

Out of Control: One Group's Story

Anne, 13, never imagined how gossip could devastate a friend. "I had a close group of four friends until last year when one of them, Sophie*, started saying mean things to us. The other two girls and I were upset, so we started talking about her as a way of getting our feelings out.

"But then it got out of control. It got pretty mean. After a few weeks, a guy in class told her we called her a really bad name. She . . . told her parents, who contacted the school. Sophie ended up switching schools for a year! I feel awful about what happened, but I learned a lot from it, too—like how badly you can hurt people by talking about them behind their backs."

*Anne's and Sophie's names have been changed. This story appeared in *Choices*, November/December 2006.

Did you hear about her?

Who Said What?

How much time do you spend talking about other people? Robin Dunbar, an evolutionary psychologist, did an experiment. Evolutionary psychologists study the way different **traits** develop in a species over time. Dunbar and his students are interested in language. They listened in on people's conversations. They found that two-thirds of the time, people were talking about "who is doing what to whom."

Dunbar's theory is that our brains are "wired" to store lots and lots of information about other people. The purpose might be to be able to tell friends from enemies. They think this may have helped our ancestors survive. And having all of this space in our brains available for facts about

No! She did that?

people might explain another one of those facts of teen life: gossip.

The Give and Take of Gossip

So science gives us an explanation for something you probably knew already: people are going to talk about other people. Let's face it, learning juicy details about someone else can be entertaining. If it weren't, *National Enquirer* would go out of business.

People are going to talk.

Gossip may be unavoidable—and even natural—but that doesn't mean it's a good thing. It may be somewhat amusing to dish dirt on someone. But before you indulge in gossip, imagine it from the perspective of the other person. It's never fun to be the subject of whispers and rumors. "I live in a small town, and people around here love to talk," says Whitney, 17, of Oklahoma. She was the target of a nasty lie recently. "I was supposed to meet the person who was spreading it after school to confront her. She never showed up."

Gossip is a problem in Courtney's tight-knit school, too. "You can't avoid it," she says. "And it's so much more vulgar now than it used to be. Most of the time, it's not true at all, or it's a big exaggeration. I try to shut it out."

"You can't avoid [gossip]."

QUIZ:
gossip or not?

1

Mary kisses one of Ashley's ex-boyfriends while watching a football game.

a) Later, Ashley finds out and immediately places a three-way call to her friends to tell them the news and to call Mary names. Is this gossip?

b) Ashley is upset that her ex-boyfriend is seeing other people already. She tells her best friend, Dana, and asks if Dana can cheer her up. Is this gossip?

2

An upperclassman picks on John in the school parking lot. A third teen, Craig, watches as John backs away and walks quickly into the school.

a) Craig approaches John and tells him that he thinks John should have acted tougher so the guy would stop bullying him. Is this gossip?

b) Craig tells people in the cafeteria what he saw and says that John is a total wimp. Is this gossip?

3

Maria, Kristin, and Jessie are the best of friends and do everything together—until Maria and Jessie get into a huge fight over which one of them they think Kristin likes better.

a) Maria tells Kristin that Jessie said Kristin doesn't look good in any of her clothes. Is this gossip?

b) Afterward, Kristin decides that the fight was stupid and announces to everyone in study hall that Maria and Jessie were fighting over her. Is this gossip?

Answers: Talking about other people's private lives behind their backs is gossip. If you share something about yourself or the person you are talking to, it is not gossip. 1. a is gossip; 2. b is gossip; 3. a and b are gossip.

Source: *Choices*, November/December 2006.

What To Do?

Experts say that Courtney's got the right idea about trying to shut gossip out of her life. Justin has a similar approach. "I really don't care what a lot of people think of me," he says. "And the people I do care about I'll talk to directly and make sure they know what the deal is."

If you are the target of gossip, psychologist Tina Tessina suggests asking yourself this question: "How much is this going to mean to me in three months?" As painful as it may be when it happens, it will pass. "Just think about how it goes with public figures," she says. "We may be hearing horrible things about some celebrity right now, but three months later, we're saying 'Paris, who?' People move on to the next scandal of the moment."

If the person who has started gossiping about you is someone you considered a friend, you may have to take a long, hard look at that relationship. A good friend wouldn't make up lies about you. A good friend also wouldn't broadcast your secrets to the school. If that is happening, let the person know you are hurt by the gossip. Then see what happens. If he or she is truly sorry, you have something to work on: rebuilding trust. But if the person minimizes what you're saying or tells you to just get over it, it might be time to let the friendship go.

?

"How much is this going to mean to me in three months?"

gossip-proof YOURSELF

Here are some teen-recommended ways to deal with wagging tongues.

Ignore it:

If it sounds like bull, it probably is. Let it go in one ear and out the other.

Don't pass it on:

Remember the game of telephone? By the time some tidbit has changed ears twice, it is probably nowhere near the truth.

Challenge it:

"That doesn't sound true to me." A simple phrase like that to a gossip is like garlic to a vampire. Give it a try. It really works!

Confront it:

If you are the target of gossip, confront the gossipers directly. But don't be surprised if they slink away or pretend they weren't at fault. The truth hurts.

Be the bigger person:

Don't make up something worse to get back at the person who gossiped about you. It will only escalate things.

Confide in someone you trust:

Vent your anger with a good friend.

your
power

your power

WHEN BULLIES CRASH THE PARTY

Becoming the Bully

Nichole*, 17, is now a high-school senior in Oregon. When she was younger, she moved around a lot and, as the "new kid," was often the target of bullies. That changed after she settled in one school for a while—she became a bully herself.

"Just like the kids who had teased me, I took it way too far. I picked on kids. I would push them into lockers, call them names, and even go as far as **humiliating** them in front of everyone by making them cry. I was doing exactly what the kids who practically ruined my life had done to me. I wanted to fit in so bad that I was willing to do anything—including hurt others.

"I didn't realize the impact my actions had until one of the kids I had pushed around came and talked to me at lunch. He told me that I was a coward and that the way I treated people was a sign of my own insecurities. He nailed it right on the head and made me realize what a jerk I was. I thought it was brave of him to stick up for himself.

"I learned my lesson and began treating others with respect and learned that I had more friends than I ever had before.

"It seems like such a cliché to say this, but I believe it is true: Treat others the way you want to be treated. In the end, it is all worth it."

*Nichole's story is excerpted from an essay she wrote. To find her complete essay, go to www.tolerance.org/teens **and search "Nichole."**

No Longer a Target

Lauren is a 17-year-old who lives in Florida. After being the target of bullies, she and her mother decided homeschooling would be a better environment for her.

"I was just one of those people who others picked on. Someone punched me in the face for no reason on a bet. I'm a quiet person. I like books. I would try to hide behind a book, but they would take it and throw it. I was teased and told I was stupid because I learn slower than others. But then I would work hard and do well in school, and be teased for being a brain. I couldn't take it anymore. I much prefer being home-schooled and working part-time. I spend most of my days around adults now."

"I was just one of those people who others picked on. Someone punched me in the face for no reason."

Beyond Bystander

Emily, 12, of Maryland, got a major benefit when she decided not to be a bystander—she made a new, good friend.

"Brianna was new at school, and she was being teased on the soccer field because of her weight. She got upset, and she rushed off the field. The PE teacher was going to send her to the office, because you're not supposed to leave class like that without permission. But my friend Caroline and I asked him to wait. We told him what happened, and we went to find her. We talked to her. We helped her not get in trouble that day, and the three of us have been friends ever since."

Are you a bully? Are you a target? Are you a bystander?

What's Your Role?

Sadly, everybody has a part to play in the bullying dramas that are all over schools today. Are you a bully? Are you a target? Are you a bystander? Perhaps you have been cast in each role at different times. The good news is that teens have the power to get out of these dramas. In the process, you can change the culture of cruelty at your school for good.

To the Bullies

It may be a shock to learn why people become bullies, though. "Bullies are not strong people. They are weak people," says psychologist Tina Tessina. "They find people in **vulnerable** situations to pick on, to try to make themselves feel stronger."

Someone who becomes a bully has often been bullied in the past. So it is a cycle of violence and vileness. Bullying may be physical, verbal, or emotional. It is a pattern of repeated behavior meant to demean, belittle, and humiliate someone.

The first step in stopping the behavior is to recognize it. Bullies often tell themselves they are just joking, or they are not really hurting the other person. But bullies should be urged to put themselves in their target's shoes. How would *you* feel to be called a nasty name

HOW WOULD YOU feel?

How would you feel to be called a nasty name, day after day?

How would you feel to be the butt of a stupid joke every day?

How would you feel to be hit or tripped or physically intimidated?

are you a BULLY?

If you repeatedly hurt another person who has less power than you have, then you are a bully. You may have more power because you are older, more popular, stronger—anything.

Bullying takes three main forms:

Physical
pushing, punching, hair-pulling

Verbal
name-calling, gossiping, teasing

Emotional
rejecting, excluding, humiliating

day after day? How would *you* feel to be the butt of a stupid joke every day? How would *you* feel to be hit or tripped or otherwise violated?

If you are sometimes guilty of putting down others, think of the impact that a change of heart would make on your school. If people are following your lead in laughing at someone, they'll also follow your lead if you choose to be kind and fair. It takes courage to change. Do you have it? It's up to you whether you have a positive influence or a negative one.

To the Targets

The world isn't fair, and being the target of a bully isn't your fault. But you may have to deal with it anyway. Here are some strategies:

"Don't walk alone. There is safety in numbers," says psychologist Tina Tessina. Use public transportation if you can, and hang around adults when possible. "Bullies will strike when someone becomes isolated. Try to use the buddy system to keep that from happening."

Use your sense of humor. Psychologist Michael Fowlin gives an example, "If someone called me a loser, I might come back with 'I think you're being too nice to me today.' It would throw them off guard."

"Take away their power," says Fowlin, by trying to ignore what they say. "They are looking for the power to upset you, to get a reaction from you. You don't have to give it to them."

Reach out elsewhere. If a bully is ruining your school life, reach out to friends from other areas of your life such as church, temple, or off-campus activities. You need a social life—but there's no rule that says it has to be in your school. And if a bully is making you feel unsafe, don't be embarrassed to get help from an adult.

To the Bystanders

If bullying is a problem in your school, you have a role, even if you aren't a bully or a target. Bystanders give bullies their power by giving them an audience for their hurtful antics.

"There's no such thing as an innocent bystander," says author Margaret Sagarese. Tessina agrees: "Bullying is not a spectator sport. Don't stand around and watch. Do something!"

What can you do? It could be as simple as saying, "Knock it off." If another friend follows your lead by saying, "Yeah, that's not cool," then congratulations! Together you've begun to help change the culture of your school.

If you have the courage to go a step further, then actively try to befriend people who are the targets of bullies. It could mean a lot to someone who is in a very stressful situation. And you might make a great new friend.

The main message experts have for bystanders is that you have the power to change your school. Who says that you aren't allowed to talk to certain people? Says Sagarese: "Who makes the rules? You make the rules! You can change them, too!"

HAZING
Bullying as a team sport

Q. WHAT IS HAZING?

A. Hazing is any kind of activity that someone joining a group is supposed to do that humiliates, degrades, or harms that person. The harm could be physical or emotional. It doesn't matter if the person participates willingly or not: it's still hazing.

Q. IS IT A BIG PROBLEM IN HIGH SCHOOLS?

A. Yes, it is. According to a recent Alfred University study of 1,500 high-school juniors and seniors, 48 percent of those who were members of groups had experienced some hazing activities. Every year, hazing leads to serious injuries, some of them life-threatening.

Q. ISN'T HAZING SUPPOSED TO BE ABOUT TEAM BUILDING AND RESPECT?

A. It doesn't work that way, though, experts say. "Hazing is an act of power and control over others—it's victimization," writes Hank Nuwer of StopHazing. org. "Respect must be EARNED, not taught. Victims of hazing rarely report having respect for those who have hazed them."

For more information on the problem of hazing, go to www.stophazing.org.

your business
and theirs

PRIVACY, PARENTS, AND FRIENDS

Dealing with Parents: Building Trust

"My dad knows my friends, so he trusts me when it comes to where I go and who I am hanging out with," says John, 16. "He gives me a lot of freedom to go out with my friends."

While most people would agree that healthy relationships require good communication, in many cases, actions speak louder than words. John shows his father and stepmother respect by doing chores. "They always help me, so I always want to return the favor," he says. "I wash the cars. I vacuum. I clean the bathrooms. I watch my little brother and sister." John takes the time to build trust with his parents, so they give him the benefit of the doubt when it comes to his friendships.

Source: Karen Fanning. "Friends Forever." *Scholastic Choices*, September 2002: 12–15.

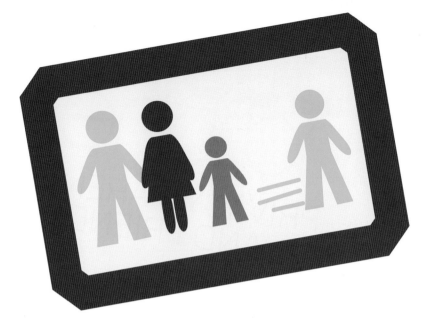

The Big Picture

You love your parents or guardians. You love your friends. And in a perfect world, your parents will always love your friends.

Well, of course, the world isn't perfect. And sometimes your parents might not like your crew. How can you deal?

It helps to understand the big picture. In your teen years, you start moving away from your parents or guardians, and your friends become more important to you. This is totally natural and expected. But it may not be easy—for you or your parents. As your parents see this shift happening in your life, they might get worried. Or angry. Or just plain nosy.

Realize this: most parents and guardians would lie down in front of a Mack truck for their kids. Nobody has your back like the adults who care for you. But sometimes it doesn't feel that way. You may want to know, why are they interfering in my life? The answer is that they care about what is happening to you and they want to protect you.

"Why are [my parents] interfering in my life?"

What Parents and Guardians Want

Do they want to know all your business? Do they want to control you? Do they want to pick your friends?

The answer to these questions, often, is YES! That's exactly what many parents want. But they also know (or will soon learn) that this is unrealistic. They need to let you become your own person, which means letting go of some of this control. Teens need and demand more independence. And this includes picking your own friends.

"Adolescence is a time when youth want more freedom to 'spread their wings,'" writes sociologist Shannon L. Sachs. But this freedom has to go hand in hand with responsibility. "As teens learn the process of managing freedom, parents need to monitor their progress. Adolescents should earn their right to more freedom. With freedom comes the responsibility to endure the consequences of choices."

"Adolescence is a time when youth want more freedom to 'spread their wings.'"

Let Them In!

Communication is the key.

The more you let your parents or guardians in on your decisions—let them see why you think your friends are cool, let them know what is happening in your life—the more they will have reason to trust you. The more trust they have in you, the more freedom they will feel comfortable giving you.

And in the process of letting your parents in, you will probably learn more about them. You might be surprised to hear about the issues your parents dealt with as teens. Or even at their job—workplaces can have their share of unpleasant gossip, cliques, and bullies, too.

Facing Facts

Your parents don't get to pick your friends. But they are allowed to have an opinion about them. And if that opinion is negative, you should really take it seriously.

If you and your parents disagree about your friends, it can lead to a vicious circle. Say you've got a new friend who got off on the wrong foot with your dad. Then your dad starts hovering over that relationship like he's a private detective or something. This makes you resent your dad. It tempts you to start lying about when you are hanging out with the new friend. You get caught in a couple of these lies, and your dad trusts you less than ever. This makes you angry and more prone to try to hide your life. Arrrrgh! Stop the madness.

Just say no to the vicious circle. Let your parents know what you like about your new friend. The more info you volunteer, the less they'll be tempted to go searching for it. And consider what your parents are saying. Do they have a point about the new friend? Are you doing risky or dangerous things with this new person that you'd never do with your old crew? You get to answer these questions for yourself. But don't be surprised if your parents are a little more on target than you might want to give them credit for.

STOP
the vicious circle

The PARENT-Child Bill of Rights

Parent's rights:

- To be introduced to your friends
- To know where you are and who you're with (including online) all of the time
- To be a part of your life

Parent's responsibilities:

- To set limits for you
- To stay interested in your life
- To provide you with safety, security, and love

Your rights:

- To have private conversations with your friends
- To have time outside of school and home to socialize
- To choose for yourself who is and who isn't important to you

Your responsibilities:

- To be truthful with your parents
- To follow their rules
- To address a rule respectfully with them when you disagree with it

When Parents Disappoint

Parents and guardians are people, and people aren't perfect. You may have a parent who struggles with substance abuse, health problems, or financial woes. Believe me, you aren't alone. Every family faces challenges, and every family has faced difficult times.

The teen years are an especially hard time to have to deal with a parent's **instability**. Part of the work of growing up is separating yourself from your parents. This can be painful in the best circumstances. But if there is nothing stable at home for you to bounce off of, it is even more difficult. You may find yourself doing more and more crazy things, unable to get their attention for anything. You might fall further than you would have ever dreamed if there's nobody there to pick you up.

But you don't have to go this route. If your family is disappointing you, try to find other sources of comfort and other role models. Your school's guidance office is a good place to begin. The counselors can help you and can also connect you with other resources in your area.

SOMEONE
to talk to

Here is a list of adults you can talk to when you feel like you can't share something with your parents:

- School guidance counselor
- Another adult relative (such as an aunt, uncle, or cousin)
- A friend's parent
- A mentor from a program such as Big Brothers or Big Sisters
- A coach
- A supervisor at an after-school job

When You Make a Mistake

Sometimes, you are the one who isn't perfect. Maybe you dented the car or got a D on your English test. Or you broke your best friend's new MP3 player and don't have the money to replace it.

Whatever bad news you've got to deliver to your parents, there's a way to go about it. If you bring it up with them (instead of them finding out on their own), they are probably going to take it a little better. Here's a script that you could use as a model to start the conversation the next time you are in the hot seat:

I've got something to tell you that you probably aren't going to like. I think you're going to be disappointed in me, because I'm disappointed in myself. Please let me tell you the whole story before you jump in.

Be sure to hit on these points as you make your case:

- What happened (give them the facts, just the facts; save excuses for another day)
- Why it happened (take responsibility; still no excuses)
- What you're going to do to try to make things right (give them your plan to make things right, like how you are going to save money to replace your friend's MP3 player)
- What you need help with to make that happen (that might be a loan so you can replace the MP3 player right away and then pay them back on a schedule; be open to their suggestions)

If all goes well, your parents will respond to your calmness with some of their own. They might still be angry, but they may also recognize and appreciate your maturity in dealing with the situation.

YOUR
WORDS:
Tributes to Friends

"Her name is Elizabeth, but I call her Izzi. Izzi never judged me. She's part of a group of open-minded people who I feel really comfortable around. They've become my core group of friends."
—Courtney, 15, Alaska

"They're just good kids. That's why I'm friends with them."
—Brandon, 15, Florida

"We have a habit of making each other laugh. That's why we're friends."
—Emily, 12, Maryland

accountability—being responsible for one's actions, often in the sense of accepting blame for something negative

adolescence—the period between childhood and adulthood, roughly the preteen and teen years

anonymity—not being known; the act of not revealing one's identity

block—prevent contact from a specific online user using a function of an e-mail or chat program

clique—a small group of people who are very friendly with each other and do not easily accept others into the group

contradiction— something, usually a statement, that is the opposite of what has been said

degrades—makes someone feel worthless or disgraced

discrimination—prejudice or unjust behavior toward others based on differences in age, race, gender, sexuality , or other factors

dynamic—the pattern of interaction of a group or organization

empowering—giving you a feeling of strength, power, and/or emotional well-being

humiliating—making someone feel ashamed and worthless through words or actions

instability—not being stable; when a person has many problems that keep him or her from functioning well

oppression—treating people in a cruel, unjust, harsh way

peer pressure—the influence of one's friends of the same age and status; can be positive or negative

primal—first in importance

psychologist—someone who studies people's minds, emotions, and behavior

social currency—one's value within a group; belonging to a certain group and wearing certain clothes might give someone social currency

status—a person's rank, or position, in a group

terrain—literally ground, land, or territory; also refers to covering a certain subject

traits—qualities; characteristics

vulnerable—easily hurt; weak

Books

Actionworks. *Teen Girls Get a Voice*. Stony Brook, N.Y.: The Get. A.Voice Project, 2006. (Available at *www.getavoice.net*.)

Desetta, Al, ed. *The Courage to Be Yourself: True Stories by Teens about Cliques, Conflicts, and Overcoming Peer Pressure*. Minneapolis: Free Spirit Publishing, 2005.

Lutz, Ericka. *The Complete Idiot's Guide to Friendship for Teens*. Indianapolis: Alpha Books, 2001.

Pollack, William S., and Todd Shuster. *Real Boys' Voices*. New York: Penguin Books, 2001.

Simmons, Rachel. *Odd Girl Out: The Hidden Culture of Aggression in Girls*. Orlando, FL.: Harcourt Books, 2002.

Online Sites & Organizations

Get.A.Voice Project
www.getavoice.net

This site outlines a character education program to address name-calling in schools. It challenges teens to change the culture of their school by challenging name-calling in a kind, respectful way.

Teen Angels
www.teenangels.org

On this site, teens teach other teens about Internet safety. Go there to learn how to be safe online or to find out about becoming a Teenangel yourself.

Stop Hazing
www.stophazing.org

This site provides information on hazing and how to prevent it. It chronicles incidences of hazing on the high school and college levels, and it provides forums to discuss hazing.

Mix It Up
www.tolerance.org/teens

A Web site run by the Southern Poverty Law Center, Mix It Up has activities, posters, and ideas on how to "Bring Down the Walls That Divide Us." You can sponsor a Mix It Up Lunch Day at your school, where everyone gets out of their usual group and sits with someone they don't know. You can also read other teens' stories and write your own to be submitted to the site.

About the Author

Diane Webber became a journalist just a few years after she was no longer a teen. Since 2000, she has been working as an editor and writer on magazines and books specifically for teens. "Writing this book was a fantastic experience, because I got to talk to lots of young people, and everyone had an interesting story to tell about their friends," she said. "It also gave me a new perspective on my own friendships from high school."

In high school in North Carolina, Webber spent time on the fringes of the popular group. "I realize now that I was valuing popularity over true friendship and that this was a mistake. I didn't really become popular, and I let an important friend slip away in the process," she said. "Now that you've read *Your Space*, you don't have to make the same mistake I did."

Today, Webber lives in Kensington, MD, with her husband, Glenn Thrush, and their young twin sons, Nathaniel and Charlie.